Fields
OF
Vision

Alabama Poetry Series

General Editors: Dara Wier and Thomas Rabbitt

Mariève Rugo

Fields
OF
Vision

The University of Alabama Press

Library of Congress Cataloging in Publication Data

Rugo, Mariève, 1934–
 Fields of vision.

 (Alabama poetry series)
 I. Title. II. Series.
PS3568.U39F5 1983   811'.54   82-16113
ISBN 0-8173-0126-7
ISBN 0-8173-0131-3 (pbk.)

For Joan Waddell

Acknowledgments

Grateful acknowledgment is made to the following publications in which some of the poems (or versions of them) have appeared:

The Black Warrior Review: "Red Bird in a White Tree" (vol. 8, no. 1, Fall 1981).

Carolina Quarterly: "Limbo" (vol. 32, no. 1, Winter 1980). First appeared in *Carolina Quarterly.* "Limbo" was reprinted in the *Anthology of Magazine Verse and Yearbook of American Poetry* (Monitor Book Company, Inc., 1981), editor, Alan F. Pater.

The Georgia Review: "Thrift Shop" (vol. XXXVI, no. 1, Spring 1982); "What Happened" (vol. XXXVI, no. 4, Winter 1982).

Hubbub: "Translation" and "Snow as Sorrow" (vol. 1, issue 1, Spring 1983).

The Little Magazine: "Late Verbs" (vol. 8, nos. 3 and 4, Fall/Winter 1974–75). First appeared in *The Little Magazine.*

The North American Review: "Flesh and Bones" (no. 267, September 1982). "Flesh and Bones" first appeared in *The North American Review,* copyright © 1982 by the University of Northern Iowa.

The Peregrine Anthology: "My Mother's Gloves" (1978).

The Poetry Miscellany: "Map-Making" (#8, 1978).

Poetry Northwest: "Expatriate" (vol. XIX, no. 1, Spring 1978); "Double Exposure," "Home," and "Surviving the Jungle" (vol. XX, no. 4, Winter 1979–80).

Prairie Schooner: "Borders," "Il Salto Mortale," and "The Season of Wolves and Names" (vol. 52, no. 4, Winter 1978/79); "Sequence Toward a Beginning," "Now," and "Vigil" (vol. 57, no. 1, Spring 1983). Reprinted from the *Prairie Schooner* by permission of University of Nebraska Press. Copyright 1983 and 1979 by University of Nebraska Press. "The Season of Wolves and Names" was reprinted in the *Anthology of Magazine Verse and Yearbook of American Poetry* (Monitor Book Company, Inc., 1981), editor, Alan F. Pater. "Borders" was reprinted in *The Poets' Choice: 100 American Poets' Favorite Poems* (Tendril, Inc., 1980), editor, George E. Murphy, Jr.

Pyramid: "Full Circle" (#15, 1982).

Radcliffe Quarterly: "Night in the Nursing Home" (March 1983). © 1983 by Radcliffe College. Reprinted with permission from the *Radcliffe Quarterly.*

Sou'wester: "Displaced Persons" (vol. 6, no. 2, Summer 1978).

Tendril: "Poem for My Daughters" (no. 5, Summer 1979); "Flesh," "Forced Entry," "White Houses and Black Roads," and "A Woman at Middle Age" (no. 7–8, Spring/Summer 1980); "Places Are Not Where We Are"

Contents

Fields
OF
Vision

Map-Making

For Paul

What we need to recognize
has no name. It is
the chart of the wind,
the chant of a stone.

So we give it a name.
We call it a map.
Even as we name it,
we know we are lying.

What we glimpse
in the eye's outer corner
is never evidence, only
more than we see.

As the sky continues
to pass, we cross
and recross our geography,
looking for landmarks.

I

What Happened

Suppose you decided to write a story
entitled *My Life.* Suppose you began
with autumn, the moon's cold finger on clouds,
the scratch and silvery click of birth.
So far so good. Seasons and years
aren't confusing as faces, their thin fabric
of irrelevant facts. Slowly you learn
craft is no more than a knack for distortion.

Only you can decide who sits and smokes,
a carafe of red wine on a tablecloth blooming
geraniums. Does that come before or after
the woman who glistens with light on the terrace,
her white silk dress, her brown eyes ripping
through flesh? When does she turn her cheek
from your kiss? Isn't that after the tumble
of Lion's Bookshop, the old man, damp hands,
how later you both stared away?

Look closer. Your dead lover is leaving you
to Brahms, red velvet arms, gilt cupids,
and you're alone. Only maybe it's earlier—
the skirl of a lake, the girl in a rowboat,
her lap piled with primroses. Before the woman?
After the concert? In the park where sirens
introduce evening as a slow tide of chill?

By now, you've understood: this story,
like all the others, isn't the one
you intended to write. You're not the hero.
These events never happened. Then whose life
slips out the door, runs down to the harbor
making its first appearance? Who
is the figure alone on the breakwater
in blowing spume, as the rescuers come
just so far before they turn back?

Naked Oddments of Night

Think of the butcher's red nightmare—
gloves of blood, white sinews knotting
his neck to his knees. Or the policeman
easing in next to his wife, wisps of fear
stuck to his fingers. How architects dream
of stresses, and black waters that lurk
under new foundations. And the lawyer,
suffocation of carbons and closings.

Think of the huge-colored dreams of children,
or the blue spaces of birds'.
Think of the dreams of a woman:
doorways streaked with shadows, paths by the river,
the open windows of trees. All the far-off cities
catching fire from the sun. There in the smoke,
her last lover is leaving again, hands in his pockets
fumbling the cheap coins of her trust.

See, she turns her dense face away,
whispers *Look at the fables I write on air—*
the sounds without names, the throwaway faces,
the unfocused scenes of my haphazard life.
In this dream, she is more naked
than the oddments of night. In this dream,
she clutches more words than she knows how to use.

My Mother's Gloves

My mother's gloves lie on her dressing table
among the jars and brushes. They look
as if they were holding her hands,
her small plump fingers, scarlet nails.

My mother uses her gloves year round to cover
her rings, to hide them from the vast brotherhood
of criminals and terrorists, and the poor.

She keeps her apartment secure with six locks,
her windows shuttered darkly from views
of the Borghese Gardens. She counts her pearls

every morning. Each night, beneath her brocade
headboard, she cuddles her pillow, rereading
expired address books, empty diaries.

By dawn, her gloves begin to feel cold.
They huddle together, talk softly
about the old days in the shop window
when anyone might have bought them.

White Houses and Black Roads

We were returning from the white house with white pillars in Hungary, where the peasants took off their caps, bowed as the big car swooped between fields of purple cabbages and silver barley, down a mile of avenue, the carriage grays racing us between the larches and poplar trees.

Or we were going to Cannes, the long white villa with its shadowed lawns high above the grass-green sea, a terrace with balustrades and deep blue skies and thyme between the paving stones, and a tangerine grove and a bed of freesias, and a gardener with a dog named Cador that I loved more than my cousin Nina.

Or we were leaving for Bucharest, the square white house with square marble rooms, a garden where blood-roses splashed up the white glare of the wall, and I fed my tortoise bacon for breakfast on the verandah where swallows nested, where once a fledgling fell and Ghiorghi's white gloves carried it away still twitching.

Or Switzerland, where at three I learned to ski and in Wengen, an avalanche just missed the balcony where we were having lunch, and in Montreux, I began to ride, round and round on a lunge rein, following my sidesaddle mother in her beige habit with black velvet facings, the instructor's eyes tucked into her jacket.

Or Italy, where the air and lake met in a dazzle that danced through the shutters and over the ceiling, and after lunch, my grandfather fed me "canards" off his coffee spoon in the dark cool room that smelled of tapestries and lilies.

The countries in color like flowerbeds, like parrots' mosaic plumage. The borders dark, running like rivers, like roads, like the sooty smell of trains.

The Day They Came Back

We taxi through a day like any London other.
Soft gray light. The nacreous pools
along black pavements gather
spring, the sky, a cloud. Daffodils
spatter Green Park on the way
to King's Cross Station. Today, no V-bombs
grind above its shattered roof. Instead sun stains,
pigeons whir between the dingy platforms,
tired trains.
              In one, I sit reading *Madeleine*,
"Twelve little girls in two straight lines,"
look up to see the column lurching by.
They hold together. Broken shoes,
or rags around their ankles. They've tied
misfit coats, ragged pants with string. By twos
and threes, they clutch in knotted hands
themselves stumbling on.
Bent heads hairless. Paper skins.
Nothing to soften over bones,
nothing to look for, nothing to look in.
Their eyes hold spaces where there once were fields.
Death met them long before they filed
disembodied by my window,
not speaking, not looking round
but walking slowly, as though
going beneath some waiting stone.
Or else where long smoke scrawls
across a vaguely pensive sky
Where have we been? Where are we now?
And why?

Expatriate

I wait inside my name, translating
myself from a foreign language
into a grammar I never learned.
I wait for the phone to ring,
or the doorbell, a letter
inviting me into someone else's tongue.
I wait for some change of tense.

Through rain's white sound
and the accents of my blood,
I hear whisperings, sly familiar
dialects of the past. For a moment,
I believe a door full of words
might open into my own country.

The Truth of Mirrors

Outside, rain on the window changes
our view of roofs to schooners,
chimneys to masts. In the mirror,
all seems safe—lamplight,
sofa, rug, our faces.
Everything in its place

but the right eye where the left belongs.
Your face becomes a montage
of moments where I've never been.
You say my features map
the long voyage here.

The cast of characters completes itself—
four strangers standing in a room
filled with distance more than space.
In the mirror, I can't name the man
whose hand I touch.

Trompe l'Oeil

I mean to write of marriage. This afternoon,
a snowstorm, the flakes steady, glittering
as an old movie set. Deanna Durbin,
cloaked in fox, sings from a prop sled,
Ivory Flakes drifting round her, back-lit.
Such snow flattens my surroundings.
Hills evaporate halfway into a sky like cloud.

I remember once you put your hand against
the painted trellis on Katherine's wall
(pale blue against a paler sky)
and pushed it open into a garden, grass
and beds of zinnias. Or were they origami
chrysanthemums? *Now we're here,*
you said, boarding the waiting train
for a beach resort or perhaps
a death camp. *You never know where
you're going until you come back
to recognize it.* Like dawn and dusk,
I thought, indigo light, the same sense
of transition, the surprise of *Yes.*

We drink tea in the café at the corner,
little crooked houses familiar
as this little square, puddles reflecting
the fountain last time too. Beyond the bridge,
the turning tide throws up against church walls
a thrash of fish, derelict tires. *It's lovely
to be back,* you say and take my hand which breaks
the hazy window with its view
of sentinel trees crossing our marsh
in lines disorderly as history.

Blue dusk sifts down. The pigeons have left
the feeder. You're in your office
and it's still snowing. As always, fatigue
distracts from the meaning of survival.
But, of course, I mean to write of marriage.

Dream Caught in a Train

Small European carriages,
thick with baskets and fat thighs,
crossing now the flat red plains
of Kansas where I've never been.
How did I learn such detail
as cows queuing up outside barn doors,
the last elms drooping over porches
with gray-green shadows, faded canvas
swings? On every porch, your face.

In the haunted scent of lilacs,
you sit rocking, looking up
at me go by in windows. What
can I call out to you now
that *husband* is inaccurate?
Brother, adversary, friend?
Your face is leaning all across
my construct of this foreign land,
America, with opaque lakes,
locked-up towns. You wave long fingers,
fill the wires with messages
of old simplicities outdistanced.

I'll never enter all the rooms
in those closed houses where you live.
This train keeps taking me no farther
than your blurred features, the words
I move too fast to hear. Everywhere
I see your face, your face, your face,
the inescapable journey we've become.

Double Exposure

1

My landscape is tundra. The distance flows
toward its beginning, and birches grow
ten inches tall. Lichens splash rust over rocks,
rhododendrons twist into bonsai. Spurting alive
in the proper season, each plant is its own act of courage.

You've always denied this.
Denied the roots drilling through bedrock for water,
the holdfasts fighting off winds that never relent.
You don't notice the small buds struggling to breathe.

In brief arctic summers, blossoms are measured in hours,
and lichens darken before the caribou wander south.
The autumn light ends. Distance keeps to itself.
Blizzard after blizzard, only pebbles flourish,
growing into their strength under the snow.

2

Once more, I say *Look at this handful of pebbles.*
These are what grow best in my country
under sunrises that all look alike
and that huge unsetting magnet, the moon.
Gravel, you say, *when there is so much else to be mined,*
again mistaking my tundra for your desert.

Listen to what I've learned in years
of inhabiting the permafrost. Pebbles live
by their own pulses, add to their density
daily. Grow skin over their substance
to hold weather at bay. Expand in the hollows
that thaw keeps avoiding. Both fruit and labor,
they flower in blue bottomless lakes.
These pebbles, your detritus, my ore.

Late Verbs

1
All I need is to build myself
a house out of your body
using your ribs for walls
your spine as support
for the roof beams
of your shoulders

it would be a small house
just one tight room to coil in
only your hypnotic thud
to ease me of questions
only the echoing boom of your voice
to remind me of silence

only you

and me
curled up like a cramp
inside you

2
Most of all I want
to weave you a skin
made of leaves lined with feathers
a skin to shield you against
the icy isolate nights
the breakfasts of stones

it would shape to you in any weather
guarding you from equators
from the teeth of sleet
a skin strong as silence

you could burrow
into its distance
and there
find yourself

unknotting
inside me

Translation

I tell you, old friend, all our talk
of my language for yours proves
it can't be done. There is no symmetry
in the syntax of needs, the tenses of touch.
Think of, say, French, that luminous skin
on few words with multiple meanings—
desire, tenderness, regret. And English,
all flavor, meter of consonants, the click
of certainties—*debts, fear, wife.*

By now, you must understand our love
was a long conversation with absences.
The grammar we trusted has fallen apart
into my verbs of distance, your memories'
inexact nouns. Conditional shrivels
to imperfect past. At the junctures of speech,
nothing matches. I think of your mouth,
and what our clotted tongues never said.

Forced Entry

Some full moons, I find myself
at my own house, a sack over my shoulder
to scavenge my future. I step over
the dog, his dreams flowing into me
with messages of wind and small wild feet.
I pause at the doors of my children,
examine their sleeping landscapes, the bogs,
and the screens where each birth is unreeled
over and over until it's forgotten.

In my own room, I inspect the stranger
in my bed. He's been there for years.
Now I enter the terrain of his night—
the abandoned track where trains no longer
cry out between broken signals
and tumbledown stations. I find
his ticket to nowhere-and-back in my hand.
I've no place here anymore.

In my bureau, drawers full of nothing I want
wait to be sorted. All I can salvage, an empty
Italian locket, a brown sweater bought by a dead man.
For a moment, the moon's face explains
but I'm not quick enough. I'm back
once more on the dark paths of deceit.
My house is stealing me over again,
the thief with the empty sack who enters
my own hungry rooms, and never leaves.

Home

1

You have believed
in a house and a country
where you were a child.
All your life, you follow
them through journals,
atlases, encyclopedias.
You dig into all the words
you can find for a clue,
questioning old records,
opening dusty accounts.
You send out inquiries,
wait for replies
which are never answers.

2

At the wrong house,
lamps semaphore messages
across the black walls
of the sky. There is always
laughter, or a mother
leaning from a kitchen window
to warm the dusk with names.
The garden is rich with apples.

Outside, you are carrying
armfuls of dead leaves.

3

Or if in a dream,
you recognize home,
it will have moved
before you get there.
Where it stood, the broken
balustrades of a terrace,
a few dark-red loops of roses
against a white wall,
a darting memory of swallows.
You set off after it,
knowing your heart
will reach there before you,
again find the site vacant.

4

One night, it starts to snow
in your bedroom. You hear
the old language again
calling to you, chants
of wild geese journeying.

This time you are happy
to lie still as snowflakes
rustle across your pillow.
When the chanting covers you
in a drift of crystal,
you curl in the space
your body has warmed for you.

As the snow keeps dreaming
its snow-dream backwards.

II

The Season of Wolves and Names

I've reached the end of my names.
My children slip through my skin,
luminous fish of my flesh, in pursuit
of their restless sea, the way of children.
The girls have woven white blossoms into their hair.
As they dance bare-legged in long grasses, petals
spin down them. The boy was born with leaves
for fingers, feet deep in the lap of Earth.
They share a secret. They know the meaning
of names, believe in the paths
they are digging through water.

With no wolves at their backs, they do not guess
how I howl all night at my wolves, how I see
through the disguise of their ember eyes, wet fangs.
Tiresias fondling the points of my new breasts
in the park. "I like this. I like this," he whispers.
Mismated Narcissus hunting me down through smaller
and smaller circles, hissing "Not you. Never you."
And Penelope, who forgot. In the whirlpool eye of the giant,
I drown endlessly.

How they crouch at my door, pelts glinting
in the shadow. How tall their tongues
flaring out of the darkness. They know me well.
I always submit, let them chase me
across the margins between my seasons
into this soundless cavern, stripped
of all names but the one they are hunting.
They have me where they want me—hamstrung, belly-up.
They ransack my body to find that last
merciless name, the one I can never say
for fear the children might hear me.

Limbo

I had come to Limbo because I had always
wanted to possess a country of my own.
Aubrey Menen

No one can come here for the first time.
It possessed us before the harsh startle of flesh,
will store our footprints forever. We travel our lives
inside its boundaries, this landscape we scour
for names to touch ourselves with. This prison
whose walls are fog piling up off an ocean decades wide.

Any escape is a thin disc of sun glimpsed
through closing shutters. Gratefully, we gather memories
like prayer beads, pass them and pass them through our
                                              fingers—
The gleam of one man's skin. Another's voice.
The open lips of leaves. Summer's ochre moon.

And always the same blood lying to the arteries
and the same eyes denying their vision
of that place where we received our enduring silver tokens,

tokens we carry so carefully along our invisible roads,
proof of fellowship, proof of passage, coins
for the guardian of that last river which was the first.

Surviving the Jungle

In the tropics, one must
before everything, keep calm.
Joseph Conrad, *Heart of Darkness*

As hundred-foot rocos close over you,
and mahoganies twined with lianas, fear
runs down your ribs, the misty sweat of jungles.
Through the half-light, everything breathes loudly.
Color offers no guidelines—the green snake dangling
from a branch. The scorpions crouched in dead leaves.
Even species is no comfort—the palmettos standing ready
to advance, swords drawn. Bamboos growing twenty inches
a day. A thorn in the thumb decays the whole arm.
A mosquito bite flares into blackwater fever.
When you fire both barrels at a leopard coughing
in the cacaos, you kill the native, and his goat.
In the rush of giant ferns, the path keeps losing
its way, mold moves in swarms, fungi are flowers,
flowers open and close broad mouths like toads.
As tapir snort through the chicle, you remember
the doctor's advice, sink down under the hungry vines.
Try to keep calm. Listen to rot swelling in roots.

Green Morning, Full Summer

Before midday blanches them
into silence,
the trees' green mouths hiss
like receding waves. Like waves,
what they say to each other
is a secret.
What they say to me
is a mystery.

Years ago, yesterday, I understood
the meaning of trees;
what they are
in the blue glaze of dawn
causes the birds
to gild them with singing.
When they put on rain or snow,
they remain naked and proud.
Their leaves use the seasons for more
than survival.

Today, they reach through this heat
with sounds from the green
hypnotic seas I've always feared.
Today, my room is a cave
carved in green polar ice.
This I can understand.

Of seasons, of trees, of my life
I understand nothing.

Recurrent City

Some days are like this,
a fall from familiar geography,
a journey in search of the missing.
You find yourself in a desert
at the bleached gateway to that city
where absences clothe themselves in flesh.

You are not astonished to see them
gather on streets and squares creased by shadows.
Waving, gesticulating, they stroll
through the silence of blue arcades and out
where white sun blinks off white walls.
Dust smokes gently around their feet.
Shapes of what they never were
drag behind them, staining the stones.

In this light, you notice they appear
larger than life. You recognize
the disappearing father. The mother
wrapped up in years made of silk.
At the corner, schoolgirls sharpen their backs.
In a small group by the fountain, wordless lovers
posture once more in the glaze of their youth.
Your dead have arrived to wander these pavements.

Drawn to return to this city, you think
of yourself as a pilgrim who travels all night
across the sands toward those dark pinnacles
spearing the sky. A moon rises in outline,
balances its black center on the silver horizon.
When bells spill their ancient tocsin,
you kneel, kiss this inevitable earth
where what never happened
keeps on and on never happening.

Full Circle

Once again, I can't remember
how I got back here, can find no clue
in bolted shutters, or the long spire
wavering in wet pavements.

Carrying my unpacked suitcase
and my illegible blue ticket,
I walk and walk through streets
leading to other familiar streets.
People hurry by me as before,
saying nothing or speaking
at distorted speeds.
I never expected to find myself
again in this sullen city.

Light slants between chimney pots,
across the awnings of half-empty cafés,
and the doorways wait, hunched up
like homeless dogs.

For identification,
I have brought three blurred snapshots,
and for comfort,
the plaster cast of a hand.

Stranded

I cannot stop remembering you I have never met.
Cannot forget how your voice sounds at daybreak
when birds slide through blue light,
each carrying its small darkness
safely under its wings.
Cannot forget the silence of your listening
to the story I've not yet made up
from dry stones and splinters of mirror.
Or how your fingers don't flinch
from what I buried beneath such brittle flesh,
calling it a heart.
When you untie the scars' cross-hatchings,
reach below my skin,
I remember you
who have not arrived, who will never arrive,
as on a beach, a whale watches with its one dim eye
the only star it will ever see.

The Lovers

Imagine a meadow,
particolored with summer,
wild mustard, paintbrush, grass
climbing itself toward the sky.
Imagine a man,
light outlining his shoulders.
And a woman.

Raised palms joined, they dance
slowly through streamers of sun.
The woman seems at home,
at ease with light.
The man steps heavily, a creature
of dark, and dazzled. They move
toward and away in silence.
Occasionally, they touch
body to body. Perhaps they kiss.
The green makes it difficult to know.

Imagine this day
will never meet dusk or the comfort
of stars. The man and the woman
will trace and retrace
their slow-motion patterns,
coming close, then turning
toward opposite horizons.

If as is said, there are seven plots
in the world, this is the eighth,
the one called the cursed.
It has a beginning, perhaps in a meadow.
A beginning, it is said, but no end.

Vigil

Now the universe itself is on hold.
Constellations creak to a pause. The days
stop trying to find each other
on dreamers' streets, where the slow *passéggio* ceases.

I am that woman who must build her last house
by this river. In my room, the long hour
of night is also the one hour of day.
I lie alone, reciting the limits
my body has taught me. Out of sight of the water,
I hear it telling itself to wait
for its own return.

I wait for the doctors
who come before sleep, forcing their own trails
through the rain, wearing green gowns over bark.
Their smiles do not fool me, nor their hands,
cold as wet leaves. This time, they may bring
the signal, the one I know by heart
but have never heard.

In the corner by the window, my last visitor
is waiting. His shadow has been my familiar.
He is utterly silent, wears light for disguise.
He waits. I wait.
This release, when it starts, will be endless.

III

Fields of Vision

I. *The Light We Leave Behind*

1

In a cave under the mountain,
the bear sleeps, curled
into rabbit and blackberry fat.
Air passes through its fur
without markings.
The bear imagines past summers,
remembers the summers to come.
Salmon are spawned, die on its claws
the same morning
in the bear's endless river.
Just as the oak, funneling rain
through harsh bark,
keeps holding the snow.
Just as night curves
and recurves dense seamless flesh
around the world.

2

Stare down the slot
in the summer trees
toward the mountains,
far in sharp air after rain.
See how the trees stand proudly
inside their outlines,
following the paths of their roots
without question.
See how the mountains coil
at their crests
with forests of cloud,
how they thrust seaward
with an ancient urge,
how they change shape as they go.
And the red doe,
standing fern-deep in her mysteries.
In every thicket, wind
spells out the names
no one can hear.

3
Birds have no graveyards,
no dead impatient to teach them
the genealogy of pain.
They accept migration as simply
as they accept the sun.
Singing because it is the season
for song, they never look
to companions for proof
of their lives.
They are their own bright arrows
as they cross over our gardens,
our careful flowerbeds.
There, we plant metaphors for ourselves
in the sparse soil of desire.
We water and weed conscientiously,
carry into our houses
our ambivalent harvests.

4
Children too live in one language,
all words sounding like *yes*.
They have no need of the complex
grammar of time, the long nouns
of place. Wherever they are
is accurate.
When fear wakes them into the dark,
they aren't astonished.
When they wake to the beckoning light,
they hear the earth humming
deep under its furrows,
its haze of grasses or snow.
And God's voice in the thunder
always makes sense.
With all their selves for companions,
they never look for more
than they can discover.
Until what they are taught
enters them and they are changed.
They begin to call distances days,
wait for them to catch up.
But the days are running ahead,
each with its fraction
of what no life can use.

5

What we write in italics
is that part of ourselves
we steal from the tragedies of others.
What we squeeze in syllables
out of our bones are the verbs
of imaginary journeys from somewhere
to somewhere else.
What we call self
is a slow grinding between tenses
in someone else's life,
between letters in someone else's name.
Or why would we wake at midnight,
sweating under the terror,
fumbling for warm flesh
to prove we lie
where we lay down?

II. *The Limits Between Day and Night*

1
The dog runs in his sleep,
decoding meadows.
The traffic grates by,
an uneasy river anxious
to flow backward
to its source.
Lie quietly, traveler,
in your unbidden life,
counting the days
left to kill.
And the legends under the mountain
which led so deep
into your skeleton,
you can't recreate the myths
of your flesh.
Instead, think how birds
use their passionate lives,
whether or not you can name them.
How they sing through your sleep.
Think too how crickets scatter
away from your feet
into their secret continents.

2
The air is filled with invisible maps,
roads for Monarchs and terns,
secret footpaths for wind.
The sun follows trails of its own.
In grass by a stream,
the spider twists light
into a net for dew
and the small fish of the air.
Watch how surely it builds
its intricate kingdom.
Watch too how the dog-fox
travels the way of each moon,
how the beaver fells trees
toward the pond.
Far offshore, whales sing
of their shapeless oceans
whose tunnels are home
without end or beginning.

3

Walk out into the storm,
the sky's despair,
the wet fingers, all
those voices.
No matter how closely you listen,
you cannot understand water.
You will stand in the air
and the waters of air for years
without names for the spaces
you inhabit, the days you deny.
Water has no need to explain.
It is the resting place between rocks,
opening itself silently
to take us in.
While we stand shivering
in our tattered lives
and the cold winds of the sea.

4

Beneath the weight of the man,
a woman's heart bends her bones.
What her wet skin receives
is not union but touch.
Her body exists outside her nakedness,
is never the body she sees
reversed in the mirror,
never the body she holds
in her mind, but a third body
with little connection.
We build ourselves
from the visions of others,
shape limbs to fantasy,
flesh to desire.
In each other's eyes, we are dreams
that do not overlap;
we never escape what we never find
inside the blood's closed circuit.
We are branches clasping each other
in a windstorm, which at dead noon, stretch
apart and remote.

5

At night, ghosts
spike through the pavement of sleep.
Into our dreams come the dead
wearing their youth like leaves.
And the silenced lovers.
And the children
in their perpetual daylight.
They have waited in antechambers
where walls collect dusk
until they are freed by darkness.
Listen.
The loosening mind whirls
with unimaginable phrases.
Each word is a flame
in this heavy air.
We touch each other at last,
flow through the stillness,
a single bright stream.
Listen again.
The sea-wind has rejected the shore.
Dawn's corners darken.
We sink breathlessly
into the cages of light
where we live.

III. *Ourselves in Sight*

1
Think of the moon
and an owl's black journey,
the small animals crouching
under that wingspan
between them and the light.
All night, little deaths flare
around us and we are untouched.
What we hear in the continuous murmurings
of lives lived around us
are the same safe fragments
of interior monologue.
What we keep near us
are the memories we can live with.
We build layer upon layer
of sediment, ashes
of journeys survived,
between ourselves and the questions
we cannot ask, between ourselves
and all we might hear.
Otherwise, how could we move out
into the murmurings and the dark?

2

The way rings of leaping fish
spread out and out
over the pond's flat sheen,
where will you be, traveler,
when your mirrors no longer reflect you?
All your careful faces fused
into one face which is not there.
No skin to transform your memories.
No eyes to deny what you saw.
No mouth to revise the stale
histories of yourself.
Your mirror keeps gathering
in its generations of dust
surfaces among which you lived.
The pale glow of skin.
The gleaming flesh,
which warmed you so briefly,
so quickly gone.

3
As we leave the caves of sleep,
leave the mountains of night,
and that clear air
which is its own symbol,
we break into splinters.
The eyes' double reversals.
The ears' whimsical choices.
The hands with their permanent coating
of fog. And all those greedy mouths
gulping tastes without tasting.
What we see is the eye's shadow
of what the eye sees.
What we hear is that husk
of silence covering all words.
We are travelers
who drift through our travels.
Where we are is always
the antechamber to where
we think we are.

4

Some night, look up at the stars.
Feel your head reeling
with spaces.
The stars need no matrices.
They do not build their truths
on the histories of others.
They have no need for names,
knowing the secret names
they gave themselves
before the beginning.
They sing for themselves
and their singing is psalms.
Then one night,
with luck as you watch,
one meteor will let go,
arch its flaming plume
over the darkness,
needing nothing
and no one
in order to invent itself.

5
Somewhere
inside the earth,
in the fire and the thunder,
everything balances
on one point.
Gravity begins and ends here
where the sightless giant lies dreaming.
We are his dreams.
Distorted, puny, trapped
in the cells of our skins,
we are his mythic reality,
visions which move
at his bidding
toward the one,
the soundless horizon.
There, we will finally wake
into each other,
past flesh, past language, past hope.
As the bear, waking into spring,
finds its way through the underbrush
into the rustle of reeds.
As the bear listens again to its river,
that white chanting
of what water is.
What rock is.
What light is.
What is.

IV

Displaced Persons

In memory of Juris Udris

They cradle ancient histories in their arms
as peace offerings, travel for years
to find a place to die.

Decades pass while they erase old letters,
unwind their clocks, empty their closets of faces.
Their pillows are swollen with echoes.

They dream in a foreign language.
They have buried their folk songs
under alien pines.

The trees of their childhoods do not forget
to follow them all night,
brushing against their tongues

with solemn branches, engraving false frontiers
inside their eyelids. When they
at last outrun their memories,

find a place to die,
forests will be waiting there to cradle
their pilgrim bones, their haunted flesh.

Thrift Shop

Even they couldn't tell you what they hope to uncover
in the cascading bins, what they want to remember
in this one smell that comes in so many colors.

They say they are looking for warmth at nightfall,
or borrowed finery stitched into a label. They whisper
they may find a new cover for traveling old avenues.

Mostly, they talk of Boston, where even air has walls,
where apartment doors have only one side. How they sleep
ready in their coats, while stairwells keep shuddering.

The wind no longer comes near enough to touch.
When they set out on the same scarred sidewalks,
what they buy never equals their hunger.

As they speak, their eyes lengthen along the counters,
ceaselessly hunting a jacket for the barefoot kid
who fished sun out of the Susquehanna.

Night in the Nursing Home

Sometimes in the dark, her faded selves
line up by the bed, staring
with opaque eyes. She thinks of herself
as a mountain road blocked by debris
or as unmarked dew under willows. She feels
her young body in late sunlight by the lake.

She imagines her flesh flaked over the city
by the harbor, knows some uneasy balance
must build between what was taken away
and how the rest learns to survive.
When the old are forsaken by houses,
where can their memories live?

The speechless learn slowly to use
the wind for confessor. The lost child
is found by the pear tree's white veil.
Now she gathers faces and voices,
piecing a quilt to soften the silence.
Gently, the dead come to visit.

They murmur *We are here. We are whole.*
One night, she will leave her astringent bed,
walk out into gold, flute-filled pastures
as though she had been there all her life.
As though all her life she had waited
to say to the angel who comes part way

to meet her *I meant to bring back more.*
All I can offer is what I cherished
before it was taken away—
a baby's chirping at dawn, a white peony,
dried blood, a few ashes, this ring.
A handful of water. Another of seeds—
relics of the life I am learning to love.

Order of Battle

Our homeland, war. Outlook, black skeletons
seethe flame. Smoke rises bitter into mornings.
Glass slashes your empty bed one night.
Afternoons, we cross London wavering
among its walls. Sky is noise, is noise,
is noise. Our voices sirens,
relentless in their only syllable.
Destruction begins after
the buildings drop. In the wrong country,
survival is always less than one expects.

Today, you are dying in Rome, Mother,
and it is still our war.
Transatlantic, we speak rubble.
What can we share of peace? It slips between.
Our decades are bombing runs, the All Clear's chancy quiet.
Saying more, the air's a vacuum rushing to explode.
This fear, ticking underground, infiltrates our blood.
Strangers to each other's cities, we keep digging
for a home among the sites we once called home.

When I arrive, you'll not be the one
I come to pardon, ask forgiveness.
From a window by your empty bed, I'll see you
wandering a scenery of gutted houses.
Small figure sifting ashes for something
moonlight might have buried there
among the angles, edges, broken streets
of this devastation we can't even call our own.

Places Are Not Where We Are

Now, dawn in Rome,
while here straight-up-midnight
as my friend from Enid, Oklahoma
calls noon which is why Enid is
Enid, not Boston, or Rome

where today you were scanned for cancer,
still not knowing what your doctor
phoned me from New York
before he flew back to Rome,
where even now, you may be waking

into pearly light over the Gianicolo,
the edges of your view going gold
with sun arriving from Bucharest,
where our footsteps wander the Calle Victorea
under a sun leaving for Rome, for Boston

in which before sleeping, I ponder
parents and children, how we learn
too slowly to mistrust the places
we pause at on our way to what we call
guilt, or hope, sometimes love,

replaced this hour with darkness
which curls around my house in Massachusetts,
murmuring at my window how recently it stared
at your tired features, bringing strangely
your face, your dark eyes alive

as these last days which slide decreasing
numbers through every midnight in Rome,
which is early evening in Boston,
where I am, where you are now,
although it's midnight, and not called Rome.

Snow as Sorrow

Always it begins as though
there were no beginning. The city
turns negative, towering white
into black skies. Cold climbs
invisible stairs of its own making.
There's some correlative here
I'm too far from seeing
to see. As why snow wanders
helplessly before it falls.
Or why my life, shrunk and raveled,
buttons mismatched, leaves
on somebody else
down that absent staircase,
along avenues, a river I don't know,
can't name even in sleep.
I watch it flapping
toward spires and small bony trees,
the milky horizon beamed with dark.
The last whisper of my mother's voice
flutters against my skin, and falls.

Inheritance

In Umbria, my mother stirs
in the earth. Like all the dead,
she refuses to lie down in silence,
her shadow folded around her.

Insistent as the sea in a shell,
her voice unwinds from the dark.
Her shadow enters my house,
filling it with her remains.

How can I tell her nothing fits—
her blankets too narrow for my bed,
her dresses too wide for my body?
Death's joke is everything stays the same,

only the price of regret has risen.
In her grave, my mother grieves
for her life's elegant design.
There will always be this between us—

the silky glitter of things.
And the voice from her shadow
which admonishes me,
its salt on my face like tears.

Two Sides of a Three-Sided Figure

. . . my own death still
a theorem to be proved.
Robert Hayden

This time of year, the stars hang late
upon their moorings, stretch taut
the fabric of the blue-black sky.

Euclid overlooked such quirks
of binary vision, graphed the world
as flat, postulating planes alone.

He seemed to think that one eye sees
precisely half the view of two.
Which may be true of lines of sight

but not my life's solid geometry.
Predawn, sight and mind at odds,
I sketch on air one incessant figure,

its third side never there.
That's the segment I can't name.

I'm my mother's daughter, daughters'
mother, angle between generations,
value unknown. Another way,

I'm at time's hypotenuse, a pause
between their tangents in my genes.
Forked by men, I see each with one eye.

There's no compass I can use
to connect my constellations,
even prove their interfacing.

Slowly light swells. Young maples
triangulate the snow. Sun crawls my wall,
a spider whose web's the universe.

Transiting day, he leaves me behind,
as he leaves upon the dazzled air
that dazzling vector only the dead can read.

Poem for My Daughters

I would come to you
empty-handed as wind,
give you untarnished
the first blue gloss of daybreak,
the masquerade of fog,
the sun's sharp bite.

I would give you light,
air for your home.

But the old dusks blur
my tongue, cling to my fingers.
Time is the mirror
where our sight is symbols.

My crescent moons,
the night is rising,
and we three are fixed to stars
burnt out before their light
could drift the distance
to our tangled hands.

Breakaway

Driving to the rink at 5 a.m.
down a cold street
huddled between its houses,
a few cars pass us,
their headlights staring
in surprise.
We speak in whispers.
Your shoulder pads rattle
as you move.

On the ice,
you break from sleep.
Pale light glitters
from your plastic crest,
your clawing blades.
You spin in circles
easy as a hawk,
shooting for the net
as though dropping
through the sky.

My sudden fledgling,
powered by the tense flat
muscles of your belly,
spurting toward the prey,
the goal,
the distance.

As we leave the rink,
dawn slits the clouds.
We buy hot doughnuts,
eat them driving home
just as the streets
begin to stretch.

A Woman at Middle Age

For Ruth Whitman

morning
she wakes with her head on her arm
her body deep into itself

in the gray light she finds
runes written along her skin
she knows she must decipher
these small arcane messages
as the day begins to unroll
its one track

noon
something got lost
or was just left behind
she has forgotten its name
if she ever knew it
besides the way back
has been obliterated

in her kitchen she sits
eating lunch among the glint of surfaces
in which she sees herself
maimed or grotesque
as in the mirrors of a fun house

afternoon
her car idles through a cycle of lights
when for no clear or foreseeable reason
she turns randy as a lioness in heat
feasting on remains

she can remember *where* and *when*
although she forgets *who* and *why*
if *why* means a certain voice
or *who* the exact shape of a face

but she remembers every instant of *how*

the light changes
she is in gear
accelerating quickly
spilling trash out of her window
looking in the mirror
for those exiles
inside her eyes

evening
for a time the children's faces
twinkled against the dark
their breath pale smoke
their hands cupped leaves

now they travel distances
she is afraid to test
and she accepts that no one
will ever live inside her but herself
packed into contracting organs
where fungus grows in the dark

the years have flickered past
like windows of a train

night
her thoughts click open and shut
then turn back on themselves
as dried branches rattle
against the windows
all night long

faces hang in the corners of the room
some of them say *remember me*
some of them say *forget me*

night whistles its sea-song through her head
as she huddles into her blankets

V

Borders

As when you wake before dawn,
still dreaming of bodies—
his body, your body,
the babies wet from their journey,
the dead in their frozen tangles.

And because you are half asleep,
you understand that we are ghosts
in each other's countries, our memories
mirror images of landscapes
we believed we had charted.

And even what we call home
is a peninsula of shadows
whose borders always defeat us,
except for those two we cross,
unexpectedly, only once.

Seven Years of Your Death

In memory of my nurse, Joan Waddell
1902–1975

In the photograph, you stand starched and startled,
holding the bored fat pony by its bit.
I sit short-legged, curly-haired, with solemn eyes.
The pony drowses. I stare past the camera.
You stare at me.

*

You unrolled your childhood
to make a tranquil path for mine, unrolled
your brothers and sisters tumbling
through Islandderry woods, you the first
to steal strawberries or row the forbidden lake.
Chance gave me you
to replace unwilling parents.
To separate the sorrows from the wounds.

*

Is it because you know I bury dreams too deep
for memory that you do not come to me at night?
I cannot bury you. Each day, I celebrate you
in water, wind, and leaves, in certain ritual phrases
and wisps of laughter, hearing in my head
the Irish folk song of your voice,
"There, there, it soon will pass."

*

On the morning of your funeral,
midwinter sunlight climbed
the gray rungs of your beeches.
Your pale house tolled its ghosts.

Beside your bed, you left
your upside-down book,
your broken glasses,
the shadow of your voice.

*

I know you better now.
You have become human.
I name your faults and you are not diminished.
I almost forgive you your absence.

But our landscape is changed.
Water hides under a skin deep as air,
wind pursues departures of its own, the hills we walked
cover their green promises with boulders.

I am left with words, their ragged testimony.

*

When stars cry out to each other
across stark gaping spaces,
their voices are only centuries apart.

The forsaken live in their own mute country
in a silence longer than always.

When I try to tell you *I love you, I need you*,
my voice never arrives.

Red Bird in a White Tree

For Philip Booth

Today, his chosen dogwood
bursts into lace. Whistling
possession, the cardinal flashes in,
brighter than blood, to pose
among patterns of light.
For this, he braved midnights
deep in pines, risked
empty feeders, held off
ice. For this, he trusted
weather.
        The bird is what
he feels himself to be.
He knows his scarlet impact
among the blossoms' foam.
The life he lives is precisely
what he means, not a blurred
photo of strange plumage,
superimposed.
        He sees
as though he learned
the fallacy of dark before
the fact. He glides
among dependable branches.
And when he starts to sing,
he is not choked
by all the slow unyielding
half-truths of the heart.

Il Salto Mortale

For Ottone Riccio

There are those who cannot imagine it at all.
They think it's enough to be up there, alone
in the spotlight, alone in the silent gasp
of eyes. They dream of the courage to travel
a single strand of darkness, an abyss of breathing.
They long to exchange weight for balance.

But for those who perform it, the center
glitters with a fire beyond passion, and the wire
is only a method. Just as the fall is its own beginning.
Just as the net breaks only bones. The jump alone saves.

They love how the air widens for them,
welcome the solitary desperation of every step,
how each muscle is its own enemy.
Time after time, tensed, holding taut, they wait
for that madness which will break them loose.
To somersault away. Stretch out and out into space.
Splinter light. Engrave their own shape on the moment.
At last, leaning into death, catch life.

Flesh and Bones

For Carole Oles

The flesh speaks
to the bones,
"I am what
is real."
The bones wait,
say nothing.

As when under the right light, or time, or cloud,
hills divulge their shadows. Bones of old rivers
running underground perhaps, or secret mines of silver.
Earth, the flesh, the sweet curves of grass,
the funneled valleys where water runs all night.
Underneath, the hills hold together, bone to bone.

The flesh speaks
to the bones,
"I live by
touching. Touch."
The bones wait,
say nothing.

When any woman curves her flesh to any man,
her skeleton curves too, but not completely.
He could snap her bone by bone, does not,
preferring the small snap of the heart.
There, blood begins iambic journeyings through
her passionate confusion of flesh and flesh.

The flesh speaks
to the bones,
"I am what
is needed."
The bones wait,
say nothing.

Removed from the verandahs, the scented teapot,
smiles and gestures, bones keep their counsel.
Rituals frame agenda for the flesh. Inside each bone,
a curving passage as precise and clear as silver.
There, martyrs make their way. There, the exiled
find at last a country and a home.

Flesh

Now I study as for the first time
this body which grows old without me.
Lie beside it, keep watch over it all night
as though it were not my body, but all the others.

I stroke the breasts' brown knots. Glide
my fingertips down the belly scar, and the groin
of so many myths. I taste the curve at the spine
where sweat often gathers, and the lips
swollen with sounds they cannot make.

I stay awake and astonished all night.

When in the first smoky light, the body takes shape,
I turn from it, already forgetting.
The way a king snake abandons her skin to a rotten stump.
The way she moves out into the sunshine,
all her new diamonds glittering along her back.

Now

The moment arrives almost like any other
except its edges brimming with more light.
Be there, as the sky gathers up its weather,
its signatures of clouds and birds take flight
until this could be the Caribbean. Sun
sweats down on beaches, white and curved
as cloud, but going nowhere. A single tern
slants east, crossing those same opaque clouds
which now say *dawn* or even *benediction.*
Waves drift in, flicker, fall back, then sigh.
The scene's a fiction
of its own making. Or yours. Or mine
who glimpsed the moment's transparent ring of gold,
opened my hand, caught hold of light, and held.

Sequence Toward a Beginning

Naushon, 1981
For Martha Collins

This island is the dream that goes on
without me. Although I return
in winter sleep to its green headlands
starred with rocks, to fields
of butterfly weed and broom,
the whinnyings from the pasture.
Although I return in summer
to size my memory to its meadows.
Wherever I am, the island is waiting
inside its membrane of light,
its ancient and nurturing indifference.

*

From the ferry, the blue coast slips behind
its fringe of sails. I turn toward
the gray shade of beech woods,
a house shadowy with the ancestors
of others. Already I am back
on barefoot paths to the First Bridge
where mussels bloom purple in the incoming tide,
and the osprey circles with high wild cries
as the marsh's green secrets rush up
to his wild pitiless eye.

*

At noon, a convoy of Canada geese
slides in on silver pieces of sky.
The children set out in a rowboat,
shadows dredging sleek water,
voices drifting back messages
iridescent and abstract as birds'.
Across the bay, they will drowse
on white sands where their forefathers landed,
while the sun moves off
with its chips of their slim coincident lives.

*

At dusk, two egrets—
white parentheses to the brilliance
of eelgrass. At my window, light
droops from the one dead tree.
With midnight, the only luna moth
I've ever seen will come back to batter
her huge luminous madness on the glass.

*

I have spent my life imitating
the songs of others, catbird
my father. I have spent my life
hungering for the nests of others,
cuckoo my mother. This is the island
of others which I now claim
for my own. I am the single crow
who digs in the marsh at dawn.
I am the boulder at the prow of the reef,
gathering a language from the throat of the wind.

*

In late afternoon, I walk
green tunnels through the forest.
Somewhere on the mainland
are men who hold me in their minds.
Here I am free
to uncover myself to the secrets of birds
who know where and how to return.
When a doe and her fawn break
through the brown light under the oaks,
I forget the seamless myth I have made
of my childhood. I forget the faces
I invented to disguise my regrets. I think
how the soul sets out on its journey from exile
with only a heart for its compass.
And I say to myself *I will live my life.*